PETER DANIELS is the author of two
pamphlets, including two Poetry Busi
single poem competitions including t
and his translations of Vladislav Kho
Classics, 2013) were shortlisted for thre
Weidenfeld translation prize. As queer writer in residence at the London
Metropolitan Archives he wrote the obscene *Ballad of Captain Rigby*.

C000007882

POETRY

*Breakfast in Bed, with Kenneth King and
Kieron Devlin* (Oscars Press, 1986)
*Peacock Luggage, with Moniza Alvi* (Smith/Doorstop, 1992)
*Be Prepared* (Smith/Doorstop, 1994)
*Blue Mice, as Peter Daniels Luczinski,* (Vennel Press, 1999)
*Through the Bushes, as Peter Daniels
Luczinski* (Smith/Doorstop, 2000)
*Work & Food* (Mulfran Press, 2010)
*Mr Luczinski Makes a Move* (HappenStance, 2011)
*Counting Eggs* (Mulfran Press, 2012)
*The Ballad of Captain Rigby* (Personal Pronoun, 2013)
*A Season in Eden* (Gatehouse Press, 2016)

TRANSLATIONS

*Vladislav Khodasevich, Selected Poems* (Angel Classics, 2013)

ANTHOLOGIES

*Take Any Train: A Book of Gay Men's Poetry* (Oscars Press, 1990)
*Jugular Defences: An AIDS Anthology, with
Steve Anthony* (Oscars Press, 1994)

PETER DANIELS

My Tin Watermelon

SALT

CROMER

PUBLISHED BY SALT PUBLISHING 2019

2 4 6 8 10 9 7 5 3 1

Copyright © Peter Daniels 2019

Peter Daniels has asserted his right under the Copyright, Designs and
Patents Act 1988 to be identified as the author of this work.

First published in Great Britain in 2019 by
Salt Publishing Ltd
12 Norwich Road, Cromer, Norfolk NR27 0AX United Kingdom

www.saltpublishing.com

Salt Publishing Limited Reg. No. 5293401

A CIP catalogue record for this book is available from the British Library

ISBN 978 1 78463 209 0 (Paperback edition)

Typeset in Sabon by Salt Publishing

Printed and bound in Great Britain by Clays Ltd, Elcograf S.p.A

*To everybody*

# Contents

# With the Mouth

Whenever you're talking, using
what's in your mouth, you don't need
to grab a scraper to understand
the barnacles under the boat, or
take a pick to the tarmac to find
where the road comes from, because

there's an implement between your throat
and teeth, a gift from your mother
who taught you to shape your world
with its edge, as she was bouncing you
on her lap, bouncing you like Moses
lifted from his basket, little foreigner.

# Buggers

Revisited, invisible inside me,
the mile of streets I'd walk home
from primary school, slouching around,
unhappy, not for years admitting I knew why
from what I'd heard my parents tell each other.
Still there, the streets, different in time,
Bournville still making chocolate under new
foreign management amid the benevolent relic,
the garden village of cottage-style houses but
the perfect cottage, the red brick gabled park toilets,
long gone: where at maybe seven years old
I opened a green-painted cubicle door to
an uninterpretable blur before I closed it
– maybe only facing one man's hairy legs, but
there was a meaning nearly understood,
too much a thing I almost knew about myself.
I knew the word 'bugger' before the word
'fuck': and on asking what a bugger was,
'They're men who touch their Mr Williams',
I already knew where this took place.

# The Break

For fathering the man, I had to call
the man myself. My throat had found that voice
but I still lingered shrilling up the scale:
a childish treble, highest in the class.
I kept the unexperienced man inside
this whiskered boy, until I'd passed sixteen.

Then it was more embarrassing to hide
the adult than admit him, and sustain
the baritone that years before began
down in the broadening larynx. At eleven
once, I'd dared to summon him, a strange
young grown-up voice, in self-defence. But when
I brought him out at last to act my age
he seemed less deep, though that high boy was gone.

# Alexandra Road

I was climbing
     that steep hill
up from my
     student bedsit
towards the campus
     as usual, but
this time I was
     exhausted
before the top:
     in early March
winter had left me
     out of resources,
dizzy. They gave me
     an "old fashioned tonic",
Orovite, sticky
     golden yellow
bottled fake sunshine,
     but it worked.
I was young
     and bounced back,
but afterwards
     I'd always notice
that time of year
     a low energy
knocked me down
     while I was climbing
up the calendar
     over again,
climbing the same
     hill that started

gentle and rose
        steeply to a flatter
top, like the graph
        of a normal bell curve,
and the campus
        at the summit
of the average.

Every year, I
        climb up to summer,
high, easy,
        warm and pretty,
for whatever it
        ripens and rots.
In my daily climb
        I am seeking
the formula
        for sun to sparkle
over the fountain
        of my average human
metabolism.
        When I've found that,
I might be ready
        to climb the crooked
stairs to the roof of
        the dismal postwar
hall of residence
        (since demolished)
to step up
        into the waiting

screw-nosed cockpit
      and fly over the town,
above the old campus,
      and off
towards the heights.

# The Chime

The chime on the door to his flat in Moseley
had a creaky lever like a knocker to lift,
flicking two notes of metal inside, as in
a musical box. Pretty, like the pretty doormat
not on the inventory, that he snaffled
for the house in King's Heath where we
moved together, and later I took with me alone
to London – where it stayed till it fell apart,
only bald bristles and a bunch of coloured rags.
The doorchime was fixed to the flat door
for visitors to ring, despite the main bell,
as the front door was often unlocked.
The burglar tried the front bell to check
who was in, and then rang the chime.
We were two men in bed unusually early
after sex around nine in the evening,
so we left it, before he jemmied the door
and entered (he didn't wipe his feet).
We could see his silhouette in the hallway,
the iron bar in his hand. I had no
presence of mind but I'm glad only one of us
called from the bed in the dark, 'Who's there?'
and the man said 'It's me,' running off.

# Selly Park

Slicing garlic, I notice how it brings into my mind now
one particular street, an unexceptional terrace, where
a young woman in the office was about to be moving
with her husband. The bathroom had been painted
with naked ladies by the current owners, two women.
This was the late nineteen-seventies. Slicing garlic
reminds me because an older woman, not unsophisticated
in an Elizabeth David way, explained to the younger one
the method of chopping it fine with the point of a knife –
not that I do it like that myself – and this would be a way
she could please her husband with food as adventurous
as their lesbian bathroom. I never saw those murals, but
slicing garlic or even onions will recall her street
along with other streets around that part of Birmingham,
and other people I knew living their own lives there:
how I knew them, food they cooked, their bathrooms.

# Days of 1985

Three years into my London life, finally
a permanent job and somewhere to live.
Still half a dozen empty houses on the street
in this inconvenient slum, with here and there
bohemian gentry: I was 31, young but not that young,
platonic shared mortgage for the flat, £33,000
(a quick sale for the vendor's messy divorce).
A group of us spent Sunday afternoons
logging and sorting newspaper cuttings
with a mention of 'homosexual' or 'gay'.
Soon the disease overwhelmed it all – 'Vicar Says
I'd Shoot My Son If He Had AIDS' – plus Boy George
got big, the other story keeping us busy.

And that Christmas, painting the living room
lemon yellow, sick of it, I went out, walked to
the Edward in Islington and met a man who wasn't
the answer but whose battered Volvo, left-hand drive,
made up for the festive lack of buses. We lasted
the next six months. He'd spent his postwar childhood
in this neighbourhood, but not-noticeably-orthodox
Jewish families like his were moving out,
the houses kept on crumbling, and the planned
Motorway Box was due to come across this street:
then didn't. By the mid-eighties, people who needed
a place to buy were moving in, and here I was,
painting the living room yellow.

# The Universal

Take me for example, a man in the street,
with my cells doing what they do with me,
molecules in the roiling swamp of my existence
like a feeling thinking walking ocean of plankton
pushing its own agenda. How can that matter
more than the single snowflakes matter
that grind against each other in the drift
to become a heap of frozen water?
These five senses, that vibrate
in their loosely grouped organs
housed in skin and bones, will
fall gradually away though I sustain it all
with toast and Marmite, mugs of cocoa
– you too, according to your preferences.

Something makes up an entity,
a human being sharing facts about itself,
its place of birth and mother's maiden name,
its tastes – maybe not its private regrets and lies,
its masturbations and adulteries –
but having things to share because it's
noticing things, what it likes about them,
which café serves the better avocado toast,
what are the satisfying shapes and styles,
why that face in the crowd, what is it
with the moon over the sea, thing of beauty,
moment of truth, excuses for the use
of the word 'universal'.

And that's probably
never exactly a lie, never exactly a fact,
but what seems to matter. And what
seems to matter about our matter is
it notices what makes existence
what it is. Non-existence must be
something else, something that's
not exactly nothing, something I'm afraid
one day I'm going to have to burst into.

# The Cave

I am the room where I work, where I fall asleep in chairs.
I live in everything in it, each thing chosen, forgotten,
and reclaimed. I'm the walls filled with books I bought
and need to read. I'm the toffee tin from Aunty Sheila,
filled with magnetic words. There's a place in me
for the old kitchen table from home, with turned legs
gnawed by our rabbit, and the nursing chair where I sat
in the bathroom when I first achieved ejaculation.
I have become my mother's armchair
(which first belonged to my partner's mother),
and my father's oak swivel chair, the part of me
in which he wrote his mathematical papers
– often I doze in one with my feet on the other,
unless I've sat up properly, up at the desk I inhabit,
rescued from my old place of employment.
My carpet was handed on from an old lover's
old lover. I'm filled with mugs, old friends,
cracked, no handles, crammed with pens and pencils.
I've been made of things I hold genuine
because they hold me. No use pretending
this is a tidy room, but I've cleared the floor,
I've made it ready for work, and at last I can say
I've started. The work will go on in this cave
till I'm done. Then I'll be free to sleep.

# Obsolescence

That was my old kitchen. It didn't take long to dirty,
but shouldn't have taken so long to clean.

There's my very first computer, the actual model
in an art installation. I gave mine to an enthusiast.

New Year. The January turnover of new leaves,
being good, from self-disgust or whatever does it.

April also is a new year. September – everything hanging
over it. The world isn't bothered when you start your life.

The outskirts of the future with its new tasks,
new objects with new dirt to clean them of.

Those floppy disks I threw out by mistake held
all I cared about at one time, but they're gone.

Those meals I made in the old kitchen,
now they're my body, my bones and fat.

# Old Beast

It's a quiet rainy morning and I have plenty
of other things to do, but after the hot days
I look at this filthy flat with enough bored energy
to grab the heavy old grey Electrolux
and get down to it.

The near-obsolete animal,
hidden in its corner for ages,
is well adapted to its habitat
as even the dinosaurs were in their time,
pulling their weight across the land,
absorbing the flora and smaller fauna.

I like gliding with that soothing to and fro
motion of the long neck and smooth head,
and I like what I can only call
the heft of it.
It's been with me thirty years now,
missing one of its tools
but instead I use another
from my mother's Electrolux
that I grew up with, still
fitting like an ancestral element
in its adaptation to deal with
stairs and awkward corners.

The heft is what James hates about the old thing
and so we bought a little Dyson, cordless,
bagless, nippy like some early mammal
in its superior mode of being:

but that's all very well, bagless means
the dust needs control at the disposal stage
(that lever and flap could do with evolving)
and who needs cordless – in this small flat,
with an extension, who even has to change
sockets? I'm not against progress, but
the old beast hasn't yet been defeated by the dust.

# Geraniums

Benign neglect has not paid off this year.
Cold and snow from the east has hit hardest
at the front window boxes. Geraniums
last year kept themselves alive all winter:
now they've turned to gnarled brown heaps.
On the other side, facing west, it's a mixed picture.
In the more sheltered bedroom window-box
the plants aren't doing badly, but at the bay window
nothing looks healthy, and favourites have gone,
like the ones with sage-green leaves variegated white
and small cherry-red flowers. I could have tidied up
in the mild spells between cold snaps, but
I've left the dead parts hanging. Face it,
the surviving plants had better be sacrificed.

Benign neglect: meaning I mean well but don't
pay attention. Procedures like uprooting
and storing them in boxes would honour
their beauty better, but it takes trouble.
One year I packed each window box with straw
and bubble wrap, but all the plants
got damp and rotted. And winter's hardly ever
as cold as this. With their strange
rusty odour, geraniums (pelargoniums if you
have to be fussy) were one flower I could grow
that didn't affect me with their scent. But one summer
the sensitivity worsened when a spirit-based
paint invaded my nose, since when
even geraniums have turned against me. Still,
I stick beside them, in my stupid neglectful way.

# Bay Window

I have no access to the back garden,
but a window like this one gets looked out of.
In winter the view is clearer: leaves in summer
fill the space and hide what will go on,
cats and foxes and squirrels trespassing over
each other's territory. Neighbours also go on,
less visible than animals, except for one
picture window without trees to mask it:
men at breakfast in black teeshirts, or white
bathrobes at weekends, the rest of their lives
open to speculation. Birds are mostly
small balls of fluff shooting through branches
plus blackbirds, magpies, pigeons, occasional jays,
once or twice a woodpecker. This window
picks up information, passing it into
the steady stream of time where I live for now,
time I'm borrowing from everyone who ever lived
or will be living after me. I take it
without refreshing the screen for them, looking
at what goes on, exercising my eyesight.
A white cat with black patches drops down
from a shed. A fox brushes through lavender.
Squirrels play in the fork of a dead tree.
Photons to absorb and interpret, next, next, next.

# Garden Incident

Now the woman downstairs with the dog
is no longer resident downstairs with her dog,
there's no longer a dog to own the garden the way dogs do,
and lately I haven't seen the man
who used to tend the garden and mow the lawn.
The garden's getting weedy and very green,
fuzzily green, shaggy with greenery, beginning to look
untidily untidy, not just a little wild.
Now there's no dog, there's no disincentive for
visits by cats, which are plentiful in the neighbourhood,
and visits by foxes, which are also plentiful.
Yesterday I watched one black and white bruiser of a tomcat
I used to see often before the dog,
as it moved slowly but purposefully up
one side of the overgrown lawn, while a scraggy fox,
I'm guessing from the wildest garden two doors down,
moved parallel up the other side of the overgrown lawn,
not in a chase but together comparing each other's progress
at not moving too fast up the garden, until my sense was
the cat was making the running, without any running at all,
claiming this as cat territory now, where foxes
have to move slightly faster than cats
and disappear with whatever grace they can manage
over the fence at the back.

# Squirrel Heights

There was a way across at tree level for the squirrels,
before some of the trees were cut – the lime tree is
back to the lollipop stump it was when I moved here,
the old dead pear tree no longer stretches that height
– though the squirrels continue whirling and swimming
round the trees, rummaging for what a squirrel wants,
and can that be nuts in May? But what otherwise
are they after? Now those fine gaps to skip
have gone, they have to engage with fences
and shed roofs in their drive to keep moving.
Once when the trees were high I saw them cross
on twig-ends, while a cat on the grass looked up
with hatred: no creature should be allowed that skill.

# The Figs

That fig used to take up the whole garden
with shade from the spread of its broad leaves.
Birds burrowed for insects and nested in the ivy
binding its trunk. From the window, I'd only
imagine its coconut scent, like the scent
by the railway, seeping from the feral fig
with its longer-lobed and gappy foliage,
no decent coverage for Adam and Eve.

But several years ago, the fig in the garden
was chopped down to a stump with one side branch
turned up at ninety degrees by the wall, looking
like a stovepipe – until today: the tidy (not to say
obsessive) gardener downstairs has cut off
that absurdity, the stump now cleanly shaped
but with a couple of neat growth-shoots
on either side. (The ivy had gone long ago.)

And the railway fig's been chainsawed down
with the usual sycamore brushwood along
the embankment by the station, to reduce
the autumn leaf-fall mulch on the track:
and figleaves would be stickier than most.
But I expect that tree to come back, as
they've cut it down before: I'd like to bet
even the fig tree Jesus blasted rose again.

# Street Trees

Trees this side of the street, lamp posts the other.
Ten years ago a small public subscription, five pounds,
got them planted, the year after I'd left my job to become
a person again, or a different person, let's not overdramatise,
not using the house for sleep then scuttling out to the train
in the winter dark and back in the dark: regaining a street
in which I was living, rediscovering the need for it in me.
The trees were a mixed bunch, leftovers looking for a street,
three liquidambars, two ornamental cherries, three
Turkish hazels, a liriodendron, a locust. The other side
couldn't take trees (phone cables following the kerb), so
they planted a new row of moderately elegant lamp posts
along the cable duct, plain and urban. The old
lamp post outside our house wasn't removed till the trees
had bedded in, and left a gap through which it's easier
to see the moon rising over the flat fronts
of the sub-Palladian houses. Opposite, they don't have
a little bracket under the sill and they lack
our incised pattern on every lintel, but otherwise
the two sides are matching nineteenth-century terraces,
the only ones round here undamaged in World War Two
(the whole next block came down in nineteen-forty).
On the thirty-first of October two thousand and eight
I planted grape hyacinths under the trees. Now the soil's
impacted, but one or two still push between the roots.
A few trees are up to the height of the houses now, or higher,
the roots are heaving the pavement, slabs awkwardly
angled, and now they're spread with leaves in autumn,
the different shapes falling in stages from each kind of tree
for Mohammed the sweeper to deal with, on our shady side
of the street in which I've found my life living itself.

# Daffodil Shield

March of the daffodils planted all along the edges,
flunkeys lining the walk across the Common
that takes me to the bus stop. What prettiness, London's

heaviness made lighter: like the primrose path
to Hell, but whatever goal we walk towards
is up to us. Interpret what you're offered

– the story I tell you, and my problem with daffodils –
but conversation doesn't mean we understand
each other's point of view, each other's flowers.

I make my metaphor my slovenly philosophy, you
make your strict sense your politics. One day,
in each other's way, we could push each other

onto the daffodils, but their weakness makes them
a shield. They guard our honour: hostages to what
keeps us back from killing each other every day.

## At the Station

A sharp morning.
On the track
half a fox, its face
and arms open
in supplication.
The back end
nowhere.

# What is Mr Luczinski?

*'Hurrying and delaying are alike ways of trying to resist the present'* –ALAN WATTS

From his local station,
taking the train in its knotweedy cuttings
to the dusty dark of the tube, this is
your crumpled uncle making his journey
through this inward-opening space,
with the clever way it zips up time.
Loving the open air, yet he is drawn to these tunnels.

Up in the control room they've spotted him
at Seven Sisters, hurrying down the dismal stairs,
his shoes finding the steps two by two by two
to the empty train already
at the platform
holding its doors but bleeping like
a bleeping bleeper echoing in his hearing aid,
so he shoves himself into the space,

the space he can occupy as a licensed Londoner,
space claimed from the crowd who are not yet there
but will be,
and now they congregate, some carefully, some sprawling,
most too big so he accommodates them in his angelic soul,
the space-creating power held in reserve for this
(mostly for his own benefit).
'Please stand clear of the closing doors,'
and they shuffle in resentfully

until they have to shuffle out again.
He must avoid the kryptonite scent, dodge
the perfumed people, and puff their air out quick
before it hits. How he squeezes past
without brushing the others – or brushes the others lightly
to make the point: they needed to be brushed past,
because their time is too long,
they must shorten it.

The control room are observing Mr L.
'What a curious way of proceeding. Are we suspicious?
Is he suspicious? What's he like?' The cameras
keep his image on file, as he dashes by
in his determined way. The files of jpegs of blurred
    suspects,
the Oyster-card records from each pass of the barrier.
He pictures his picture as he passes, he can be self-
    regarding.

Mr L incorporates the journey in his physical form,
his anatomy plans the route.
'I think he thinks he's the map.'
'More like the clock, the way he
watches his watch. He's in a tight relationship with Time.'
'Tell them to get a room.'

He's unable to be all forms of transport.
He's not a tram, though he feels affinity with trams.
He isn't a moving bus, nor a floating balloon,
though he has known and loved men who were

each of those things.
'He thinks he knows where he's going.'
'Well, if that's what he thinks . . .'
He must observe the announced delays to the District,
they may impede his progress.
He has learnt to deny himself the patience of waiting
but he knows not to change plans too often.

Above him, the city keeps moving in its disorganised way.
His own measures are incoherent but generally logical.
He depends on knowing his position, the reading
of his trajectory from Rectory Road to (say) Earls Court,
Elephant, Leytonstone, wherever – Cockfosters –
navigating through the inner surface of the system,
yet he can be happy with the flow:
the escalator is his chosen medium moving down
or upward between states – lifts may be faster
but they're batch-processors you have to wait for.
If he must, he can rise with them through gravity
absorbing the inertia in his body, and so,
as the control room are changing shifts,
they stay to watch him emerge at Russell Square
becoming one with the barrier:
he touches his Oyster out, and it
lets him into the world again.

He continues his journey at street level.

# A Moment

A pork pie or a piece of cheese with his cup of tea,
a moment of calm, he can spend it how he pleases.

Absent-mindedly fondling the umbrella, upright
between his legs, while he admires the place.

Taking the moment, its applause or blasphemies:
being a human being, no furbelows or bluster.

The odd effect of light on the ceiling, the high
windows, the notices stating management policy.

Billstickers have made a mosaic of the wall outside,
the radio mutters traffic news, the fridge pulsates.

Everything is here for when anything needs to happen:
the cloudburst of witnesses, the chariots as they blaze.

# Almost Christmas

Almost Christmas and we're going home
full of a satisfying dinner and wine, but it's
office party time on the Docklands Light Railway

and at every station groups get on,
not uncontrollably intoxicated, perfumed,
postmorteming the evening with hilarity

especially this bunch braying and screaming,
so I've turned off my hearing aid (fogey's comfort)
and we've moved further up the train to avoid them,

then you get on, three men maybe mid-twenties
and you interrupt each other, each time louder and
louder till if you don't shut up I'm going to

charm you into letting me approach to get
a word in disarmingly, I'll say excuse me and I'll
shove your Santa pompoms down your fucking gobs

to show I'm so much nicer and persuade you
that politeness is the adhesive that connects
our civilisation with itself, its reasons, its passions,

its acts of gestural complexity that complement
each other, build the mirrored ballroom where
treaties can be signed and worlds made into

other worlds that always will turn out to be
the very same one because we can agree on
what we want, if only you would shut your face

because all our faces will be tiny pictures pixelled
somewhere in the billion billion billion moments
history won't ever be bothered to retrieve

when we've all stuffed each other's mouths
with the disturbed earth we stand on, fall on,
go back into after all's been said and done.

# Bunhill Fields Quaker Burial Ground

*'The Kingdom of Heaven did gather us and catch us all, as in a
net, and his heavenly power at one time drew many hundreds to
land. We came to know a place to stand in and what to wait in.'*
                                    FRANCIS HOWGILL, 1663

No, not the one with much-visited
Blake, and less-so Defoe and Bunyan.
Behind a block of flats, this is

like the not-too-obvious
place they hid in the *A to Z*
to catch out plagiarists:

as if it only exists to the ones
who make their pilgrimage, or
walk their dog despite the sign

telling them not to. And it isn't
*The London Nobody Knows*, there's
nothing nobody knows, it's always

somebody's secret, but people
who have discovered places
suppose them entirely their own.

People do own it: the man who
began this is buried with twelve thousand
followers over a couple of centuries,

with their silent truth crammed into
a parcel of land between buildings
until the charm of the place

has grown heavy with mystic pressure.
Those enormous plane trees that
have fed on all the quiet human dirt,

the screams out of the playground bouncing
back from the tall flats, the young men
who drink and smoke on the steps

of the meeting house – all want
to show you it's theirs, but they
can't hold you to account

for how you walk, stand, sit
and wait for the light as it emerges
through the city air and the trees.

# Bearded

Was it because my chin needed it? Was it who I
wanted to be – or was it who I wanted? Was there
a beard in the perfect world attaching itself to my face?

I shave down my cheeks to shape it vertically,
one razor-width, my trademark. I trim when it's
too fuzzy. 'Your beard's bigger. Have you got
a second piece of beard?' My aunt is
bothered with beards, maybe she's trying
to distract herself. 'I'm frightened. Is this the last day?'

Generations of gents' hairdressers:
Italian barbers, Afro-Caribbean, Turkish,
and now on the High Street it's hipster barbers –
*You grow it, we mow it:* they might like my beard,
and I did start twirling the moustache,
but grey's not their colour, and I'm not tattooed.

'Have you got a purple hat?' My other trademark
is cheap trilbies: I visit her wearing the purplish plaid
with a gold fleck, bought on the High Street
at one of those shops that sell buckets and brooms.

I like to walk the street on one side, from end to end.
Psychogeography attracted me at first but
while I have my obsessive ways with streets
I don't do their dérives and purposeful driftings.
You might need a certain kind of beard for that, perhaps
tattoos, definitely hats. Oh, fuck that flâneur stuff,
you with your fake Baudelairean persona.

Some beards you can recognise. Yes,
I walk the High Street, give my opinion on cafés,
a man with a beard and a hat, out there
drinking a black americano, eating a pastry.

'Do I have a long beard?' asks my aunt. 'I'm bad.'
'No, you're good.' 'I wish I were. That's
the subjunctive, you know. Where am I?'
She's not yet ready to give herself up,
life being who you are. He's who I am,
taking in the High Street life, stroking his beard,
placing his selfhood there in the moment.

# Zsa Zsa's House

Zsa Zsa Gabor's former Palm Springs retreat
is up for sale. Walls of floortoceiling glass,
exposed beams and flagstone flooring.
A lone bedroom, an updated kitchen,
living room with a stackedstone fireplace,
a swimming pool, desert landscaping, outdoor fire pit.
Zsa Zsa's well-appointed house is mid-century modern,
perfect for a few of those vintage nineteen-sixties
Danish splay-footed coffee tables that London hipsters
are sourcing in neglected provincial suburbs.
Meanwhile, here we are, nestled away from the hustle
and the bustle, footsteps from Stoke Newington's
eclectic mix of boutique shops, cafes and pubs.
From our mid-Victorian house we can enjoy
the many bus routes, and trains twelve minutes
to the heart of the City of London.
Zsa Zsa's house is in the *Daily Mail*: 'Now fans
have a chance to snap up this piece of Hollywood history
– just two hours from Tinseltown – provided they can stretch
to the nine-hundred-&-sixty-nine-thousand-dollar price tag.'
Set in a third of an acre, but it's not much bigger
than a terraced house in Stoke Newington
which is valued higher! We're rich!
We don't even have to make-believe,
some of us bubble-dwellers of London
sitting here in this impossible metropolis,
floating into nowhere in our money balloon.
The story's wrong but we're ahead in it.
Dickens wouldn't know it, but he'd know how to write it.

More than half my life ago, I came from the Midlands,
London as unreal as my provincial suburb is
unreal to me now. In our living room
we'd watch Zsa Zsa Gabor on 'Juke Box Jury'.
Our nineteen-sixties furniture smelt new from the factory,
then hung around looking out of date and silly
but still with a style to the simple lines.
The future was simple then, before neglect and decay,
and neglect of neglect and decay
left the country with a heart of nothing.
Heart of England, what's your story? Nuneaton's own
George Eliot could have written this. I'm not
the Zsa Zsa Gabor of Stoke Newington,
my fabulous home the star vehicle
for this comedy of gentrification.
Turn the page, reader. Write your own beautiful house,
your own longing, your own anger, what's real to you.
Write a part for you, a part for me,
a part for Zsa Zsa Gabor.

# Winchmore Hill

If it was me I'd call the cops,
there's no way out and no way in.
I don't understand what's in the shops
and the luck isn't good and the wind is ill:
can I get back to Winchmore Hill?

Everyone here is queer or worse,
even the vicar is ugly as sin.
Little old ladies will snatch your purse
or make you a deal for an all-night pill:
can I get back to Winchmore Hill?

There's nothing to see and less to admire,
you can play to lose but there's nothing to win.
The rainbow has melted, the clouds are on fire
and the people are coming with buckets to fill:
can I get back to Winchmore Hill?

Thank you for taking me down to the place
where angels have sex with their next of kin
and the saints get high in a state of grace,
I'm a middle-class gentleman out for a thrill:
but can I get back to Winchmore Hill?

# A Teasel

Excuse me, there's a teasel
growing out of your grave,
and you don't even know
you've been buried there.
Taller than you, green and alive
with outstretched leaves like angled arms,
it's ready to flower and seed.

And a teasel happens to be
growing out of your grave
because you feed it.
Now it's what you are,
unashamed, the epitaph you deserve,
the burr, the scratch for your itch, a prize
catching the attention you crave.

# My Tin Watermelon

Once I bought a watermelon
made of tin, and a bunch of grapes,
a fish, a parrot, a heart, a red
crescent moon, and a shooting star.

I still have the others but after
Christmas, with the tin things
taken off the living room yucca
which they had been decorating,

that watermelon disappeared,
possibly among the old cards
also on the table, but that's only
a theory. This is serious: another

thing disappearing unannounced
into the unknown, like the trowel
from the indoor garden tool set
that belonged to Aunty May, or

the little mustard spoon from the
bakelite cruet that I knocked
off the shelf yesterday – now I
don't know if the spoon had already

gone or did it shoot under the fridge
or into that gap we can blame for
absences, drops, carelessnesses,
disappearances: like others that

have gone from my mind till I
miss the thing one day for some
reason, as I miss the things I've
ruthlessly got rid of because I

hated them, or thought I could
do without; of course, the hatred
and the needless need are
what I miss. Gingerbread tins,

honey pots, books I disliked and
want to revisit for why that was.
A useless thing is still a thing
and has its ornamental reason.

Seven tin ornaments, chosen
as two animal, two vegetable,
two mineral plus the heart
(the abstract shape); I'd wanted

to make the set into a mobile,
one of those intentions never
realised. Now only six, less
magic to hang above my desk.

I don't even like the flavourless
flavour of watermelon but
a tin watermelon hanging
in the house, that's a thing.

# Roses

You can't abolish roses. Their scent means the whole
world  gets into your nose. They're a vicious origami,
layered, tightly bound, then as they spread they hold you,
till the petals flop. They may have to be your mother.
Roses can destroy you if you fail to achieve oneness with
their all-embracing point of view. You need guts to deal
with roses. Where did they come from? Like everything,
they floated on the Gulf Stream, or they arrived with the
Romans, or the birds flew by one day with rosehips in their
shit. That's not so important. But they'll find you.

# Out of the Box

On the street I grew up in – an old road between villages
strung into a suburb, in rows of clumped nineteenth
and twentieth century styles – our house was the last one.
I'll still be part of that street till it's all we've got time for.

All we've got time for because our veins will narrow,
bodies shrink, houses tumble into nothing until
the spell breaks, and the world is a piece of dust
still rotating, but now time is out of the frame.

Out of the frame now and into sublime abstraction,
more sublime than ever without the somebody there
to think of it, licking a frozen orange juice on the way
home from school, down the street I grew up in.

∼

And that's that closed. Every box has an outside
and an inside, and words can make boxes to hold you
in their little contraptions like mine, wanting to order
the way you live: but okay, you'll be the judge of that.

And who's to be the judge of what is the case, of your
factual existence? How could you tell that this world
was lovely, and will it be again, ever, once it's settled
the giants are in charge and the genies out of the bottles?

Out of the bottles, too, our lost breath and the blood
sucked out of us, whether we're embalmed or incinerated,
nobody there to believe that this was our box, our street,
our frame, our time, and the case on it all is truly closed.

# Trajectory

If you can trace
       a soul's journey,
there it is,
       setting out now
from the house
       where I was born,
past what we called
       the Slippery Ditch,
across the railway
       into the unknown region:
to start meandering
       from point A
towards the distant view
       of point B, over
wooden planks between
       the stretches of rushes
and sedge, past winding
       pools of sludge
impossible to map.
       Occasionally,
small birds flit and tweet.
       My soul has no
reason to move
       around the map,
but wants to be
       left alone with
the local geography,
       hoping to find
a bridge across
       the slimy water

and a tolerably solid
        island to land on.
The wandering bog
        is almost featureless
and that's its glory, though
        there's also a cathedral,
built on an island:
        you can't miss it,
complicated, pointed,
        spectacular.

# Haddock Breakfast

The wind pushes
and the water rides along till it falls onto the stones.
Each wave a different thrust, then the pull away.

Wind and foam work at the edge of the sea,
sand and shingle wait at the edge of the land.
Shingle slows down the feet.

Windows face it out along the hotel front
where we sit at breakfast, watching the sun
pop up over the horizon.

Concrete steps of local lime
mixed on the spot with native shingle
hold up the sheds: Fish Smoked Here.

Local haddock with bold poached eggs:
from the sea where haddock are fished,
from the land where eggs are laid.

My heavy tread on the shingle
has trudged along a street once there, no longer.
Nothing can wait forever for the likes of us.

The sea we once came from
spreads around us. The land we come from
shifts and settles.

The shore is as far as
anyone can go on foot,
or come by boat.

The comfortable hotel: in a hundred years
bashed to a hollow cliff of bricks.
The future shared between gulls and sparrows.

# Riff on a Line of Miłosz

I was afraid of what was wild and indecent in me.
No beginning to the thread I found through the forest,
the creek full of excrement – I mean, shit – and then
where I emerged squeezing through the crush of bodies
I was unsure which part of the station I was in.

I was afraid of what was wild and indecent because
it was mine, and especially of what I'd seen once
at the toilets in a half-known part of the station.
I could guess where the creek was coming from
and where it would go through the raging forest.

I was afraid of what was wild in me as if it would
kill what I'd found indecent and beautiful, which
was only what the bodies of people, afraid, wild
and indecent, full of shit, piss, blood and semen,
could build out of pieces of wood, bones and dust.

I was afraid of the wild rush of water through the forest
approaching the creek from the high path too dark
to see what I might fall down into. Afraid I had to
reach the gate before nightfall and show my papers
to enter and enjoy the indecent city of toxic lights.

I was afraid of what was wild and indecent in me
yet I could find it when I needed it to hustle me
onto a train through the forest, and give back my self
new and dirty, a small stain on my soul to be kept,
stroked, and made into a badge of my allegiance.

# King's Cross

I don't remember their tune, the buskers
who stood at the bottom of the old wooden escalator,
squeak-scratching fiddle and accordion chortling,

but fifteen pence I remember I gave them
for my passage up to the surface,
the morning before the fire.

# Answers

I'll tell you what happened, shall I? You lost
your ring at King's Cross, in the canal. A fish
found it and swallowed it, I caught the fish
and now it's time to cook and eat it, but you
won't believe me when I show you the answer.

Man on the train has lost his cherry from off of
his Belgian bun from Gregg's, it's on the floor
and he hasn't even noticed. I'm not going to
tell him, 'Ha ha, you've lost your cherry': what
would be the point, as he can't eat it anyway.

I have nothing to tell you, now you've lost your
way, no special treat, nothing you could swallow:
nothing will come of nothing and why would it,
it's never a good time for truth now the gilt
is off the gingerbread, no one wants to know.

We get to King's Cross another time: I could tell you
where you need to go, but it's all so confusing
and you can't get anywhere without having to
ask all over again, though you'll be too proud
to ask, like most lost men, who won't be told.

Your lost cherries and unvarnished gingerbread might
have been the answer you didn't want to ask for
but you want the answer you want, not to be shown
what's true. You dropped your ring and now
the fish can't even be bothered to swallow it for you.

## Lost Property

So I've found this perfectly clean pair
of underpants, though they aren't
new, in the toilets at Cambridge station
– that's the old toilets before refurbishment,
with mirrored walls, four walls of mirror to each
cubicle, a wall of mirror behind the urinals
but not glass mirror, some kind of mirror-surfaced
laminate which makes the entire Gents a strangely
theatrical experience, and so it's unsurprising
to find this pair of underpants, Calvin Klein
though not the classic white, and not boxers,
a kind of shorts with a graffiti pattern
along the elastic: seems inappropriate to
hand them in, no way of tracing
the owner, they're definitely clean,
they fit, I take them home.

# Catalogue Man

Look at him in his black silk longjohns and top, what is he,
some superhero? Where are his superhero boots, and panties
over his smooth crotch? What would be his superpower,

undisclosed, locked in till he needs it, like the snug penis
and balls waiting to bounce free? What kind of supergizmo
is kept back before we see him save the world, by virtue

of his black silkiness, that moment he lets the special device
shoot out, his supernaturally extensible plot resolver? Or
is there nothing unusual about this man? Sometimes a penis

is simply a penis? What gives black silk its power to enhance
his own power, what fascination – sheer charm, darkness?
Black silk longjohns man in your underwear catalogue,

what are you really offering? What terror lies hidden? What
delight? Why do I want to taste your unattainable secret?
How would I look myself in a black silk longjohns outfit?

# Go West

Each range its own challenge: the badlands
where canyons cut deep across the high plains,
the snowy peaks, the desert, and California
tumbling its gold. The land itself breeds
cowboys like cactuses. They rope and roll,
roostered at the end of the day. We dream of them
back East in our overpaid featherbeds. Farther
out on the fantasy coast, they make it happen
on the hilly backlots of Hollywood – what they can do
with a ropehorse, a gun and a basic plot
with bandits in bandanas. 'We'll Westernize you yet!'
said Richard in the thrift store in Hippytown
trying me on with a puffer jerkin over my denim.
This far West the rules change. Get a load of him,
he's got the attributes to get himself laid
and get seen getting laid, sex for downloading,
body pumped and swollen inside his leather.
What he can do with a cowboy hat and a banana.

# Blood

River inside me that
        I need to keep
                flowing, unspilt:

when risk breaks the barrier,
        blood will be where
                the infection appears

– which it didn't for me
        but could have done.
                The thin wall of

rubber kept the blood
        of penis and of rectum
                separate. His blood

he had already taken it
        into, and didn't care
                but did care, it was his

way to punish himself.
        He knew I wasn't
                like that, he didn't

expect my own self-
        destruction in his
                need for sex, although

the pull was strong
and we wanted to
fuck each other's brains out.

But as ever, my restraint
could save my blood while I
could never save his. We were

in different places on the map
of what the world could
offer us, what we could do

to the world with blood
filling a penis, blood of
the river of being alive.

# Find Me

'Find me like a banknote in the street,
                a sudden thought,
find me
            in the spare bedroom: now
I'm this butterfly,
            red carpet-patterned,

I'm an extra guest where you'll be sleeping later.
        And you don't yet know
it's me.
            You need to let me go, but not
out into that empty November.

Perhaps at bedtime you must think I'm gone,
the way they say
                the dead are "in another room"?

Or you forgot.
                You don't know I've been hiding
while you took yourself in hand
                                    – then
I flit down on your open laptop with my
light touch,
                my way of turning up,
and you remember how you wanted me.'

## Bottom Drawer

The bottom has fallen out of my bottom drawer, the one
stuffed with forgotten trousers, pyjamas, thermal longjohns,
and a few things I'm not ashamed of but won't make public.
The chest of drawers is old and cheap, the wood inside it
rough, and warping under the weight of clothes. One panel
from the base of the bottom drawer is out of its grooves,
and bent. So much in this chest of drawers, too many
sentimental teeshirts I never wear, special underpants I
needn't find occasion for. Now I've cracked the bottom
   panel
when I tried to fix it, and we're almost out of superglue,
my only resource for mending. Some of the clothes
I've weeded. I imagine some gone but I can't see myself
never owning them. It's an old chest of drawers that
wasn't even new when it stood in the room I was born in.

# The Dream Rooms

It's evidently a common dream, the extra rooms:
looking-glass rooms and rabbit holes for Alice to explore
– but the rooms are exploring us. Inside my head
I have the means to take over the flat downstairs,
finding convenient new ways down there, but also ways
up again into a flat I don't own at all, like a bridge,
with someone else's red sofas and chairs painted white.
Or there's a different house I used to live in, and yet
it's not where I lived: there's an upstairs room,
wrecked and abandoned, plaster fallen everywhere
– how do I mend it? The neighbourhood is familiar,
though it isn't. I go out into the streets, among houses
made to live in differently, made for the dream.
'Drink me,' says the dream. I can open the world up,
pioneer every home, every room in my mental
space, like America sliced and diced into states,
the memory and the invention spreading new forms
of Birmingham tinged with Reading, or
Stoke Newington, naturally, but Coventry also,
or through that door now and then it's Edinburgh.
While I'm absorbed in these spaces,
things come right by being wrong, as
Alice could have told me. I am not to go
into that room, yet I have to, and I will.

# Home Truths

Here are the woods, managed by a skilled crew,
and one good straight birch picked out
with a red stripe — is it condemned or chosen?

Here are the characters: the magpies check out
glitter for the nest, the crows fidget in the wind,
jays drop in like big pink toys on a visit.

Here, as if it mattered, the groceries listed
and followed round the dull little supermarket,
every one crossed off, glad to be of service.

And the house in the woods, like a scene of crime
as usual. You have to find things like soap,
and gold, and logs for the stove, but it's home.

# Vegan Rhubarb Pavlova

I take my pleasures gently, like a lotus
opening for the world to enter me,
and share its own sweetness, in its passion
to seek out my desire and gratify it.
What joys am I after? I'm longing for
another spoon of my pudding at Mildred's.

Ruby rhubarb poached slowly, tender
but ridgy still, nestling in real meringue
with no eggwhite – it's built out of the juice
of chickpeas – and they've whipped up coconuts
into a cream to splurge inside my mouth,
filled now with the pudding at Mildred's.

Dinners for occasions, intimate evenings
with ingredients out of vegetable love,
fake but genuine, make the moment perfect:
the facts of the menu tested, spread out
satisfied and asking was that as good
tonight as your pudding at Mildred's?

And so I ask myself, have I satisfied?
What have I done for the world? Yes,
I'm alone in it, we're all alone, we're
grabbing hold of the last stick of rhubarb.
We've paid for that party now, our minds
lingering over that pudding at Mildred's.

# The Usual

I love their coffee, though the comestibles aren't
up to much – damp and sticky bought-in cake, pastries
better but no character, so usually I get a bacon bagel:
the paradox that's me, half-Jewish, half not, and really
not at all. But my Jewish father loved his bacon,
and the local grocers knew to slice him smoked back,
at number 5. Every Thursday the usual man asks
'The usual?' – this week I say no, I'll have a croissant:
he seems a little hurt. In fact, last week his stand-in
served me a much juicier bacon in the bagel, but
being asked 'The usual?' is so pleasing. The journey
is part of the ritual: train two stops to Stamford Hill,
a 253 up Camden Road – the 253 I first took
with my sister and Aunty Sheila the other way,
from Manor House to Aunty Fay's, with Aunty May's
collapsible dressmaker's dummy in a woven rush suitcase
that almost tumbled off the open platform of the bus
taking the turn into Amhurst Park entering Stamford Hill,
where men in black wear hats that identify who they are,
and I feel I shouldn't wear my cheap black trilby
with a black polyester raincoat, almost close enough
to be confused from a distance – yet why should I not?
In Stamford Hill the confusion's mainly mine,
awareness of a foreskin that can never belong.
I'll never have the instinct for what Jewish is,
and never give the right answer on Israel:
on which even the unelaborate Radio 3 news
– my news ritual, one more way I'm now my father –
brings news that never sounds good to me,
and seems unlikely now ever to be good again.

# Aunty May's Party

With a ballet dancer and a bishop,
      the conversation gets lumpy,
but we don't need to communicate,
      although our glasses are empty,
and all the time it's a meeting
      of scissors, paper and stone:
      *partying at Aunty May's,*
      *waking up alone,*
      *like waking up on the other side.*

The guests are highly erudite,
      with all their PhDs
costing a hundred thousand words
      and scraping together the fees,
and now they don't want to talk,
      but browse in her volumes of Proust,
      *partying at Aunty May's,*
      *waking up in the past,*
      *waking up on the other side.*

Nobody told you the formula,
      nobody offered you space,
it doesn't help to get shirty
      when what they don't like is your face,
but you've sacrificed your art
      along with the horse it rode in on,
      *partying at Aunty May's,*
      *waking to the wrong decision,*
      *waking up on the other side.*

Waking up on the other side
       is waking up in a dream,
and every word you've written
       was a stake in a pyramid scheme,
when all it takes is a sharp felt tip
       and a blunt message on a wall,
       *partying at Aunty May's,*
       *not waking up at all*
       *and waking up on the other side.*

# Pears

And that stewed pear
                vindicates my mother who told me
pears will make you pee,
                and they do, yet I keep forgetting.
You don't need to know,
                but I was up more than once in the night,
which my prostate medication
                is there to prevent, but I'd say
no blame for the prostate,
                it's only a spigot, while surely
it's the kidneys – a diuretic makes them
                squeeze more out of me. With tea
I've learned to insist on a biscuit
                that soaks it up in the stomach
and slows the micturition –
                and this works, although I can be
too embarrassed or thirsty
                to ask for one when tea is offered.
I told the Urology man, who
                was taken aback that coffee, with more
caffeine, was less of a problem.
                I didn't mention pears and, as I say,
I often forget about pears.
                James (the stewed pear was delicious,
honestly) doesn't find they do it,
                and the quantity of tea he drinks
straight, no biscuit, is even more
                than my late mother drank, but do pears
and tea contain the same
                water-making ingredient? Why was she

not concerned about
        the properties of tea? Is there a gene
for pears-make-you-go?
        On Google I've found almost nothing
except for people
        happy that pears are diuretic
for losing them weight.
        That's not the point. But by my time of life
empirical evidence makes me
        take care with pears, however delicious,
know myself, listen to my mother.

# Vertigo

Everything is moving past me to
    the right when I know it's not moving
        at all but everything dares me to catch it and
            pin it down put it in an album and sit on it keep it
                in one place but I can't because it's all in my head
my eyes are telling me it's
    moving and when I shut them
        the after-images are going round
            to the left yet this too will pass although
                it could keep passing and the world
become a river in flood ever-rolling
    holding branches logs rafts with chickens
        goats plastic balls lost dolls dead deer and
            everything moving past banks of green willow
                gorges of limestone embankments of granite
glass and steel buildings cheesegraters shards
    this city of empty reflections past all of it and off
        into the wide open water that rolls pitches heaves
            out of the world's own spinning its wind and tide
                swirling and swilling round the inside of my head

# And to Die

*'And to die is different from what anyone supposed, and luckier.'*
WHITMAN, *Song of Myself*

I see he wants us to be glad of the earth.
I shall be surprised, even so, when
I am no longer my self.
I open my heart to another breath where
I know this privilege attends me and
I find the gasp again till the final attempt.
I swallow the last of it.
I find it gone.
I have no place to remain here,
I catch the end
I could not stop for.

# A Father's Body

I'd like to claim my father, as I'm his
continuing body: not quite his face,
but more so when I put his
hornrim glasses on. I didn't inherit
his baldness, which I regret: I'd like
to feel my palm on that smooth head.
It's not his brain I think with,
though I was formed by his, and
his education. I don't speak
with his dark Scots L,
last element of his upbringing
still in his mouth. Do I have his
penis? There's no evidence.
I do have a foreskin, which
he only had one week. I'm now
about the age he gave up smoking.
I stopped half my life ago,
but when I see that now rare
maleness, a cigarette held
between lips, I see his: which
I used to see from the back seat
in the driving mirror, and I'd
watch his eyes, the eyes I
watched when I watched him
dying. Not my colour, but
the same prescription.

## The Armchairs

Now they're on their own, where
no one is sitting: no one much
has sat in them for years. One,
once rescued from the room
of a dead mathematician, needs
a cushion to mitigate its rigidity
and yet the curve is elegant. The other
came from an uncle's furniture company
ninety-nine years ago, a wedding present,
dumpy and yielding but still buoyant.
No one has decided what to do about
who they are and where they might
find themselves. They never really did
go together, but still, here they are.

# Sun in December

That cold glow in the sky slides down while the earth
is rolling back, to leave this place in the dark
and the sun will warm somewhere else, now.

Between my being born a mile away from here
and my mother's dying on the other side of town
there's been so much spinning and orbiting.

This town is like a wheel: its radial spokes are not
the route I need from the inconvenient station,
making me zigzag round it to follow my own way.

A plane makes a slight rip in the sky's empty surface,
lit by the setting sun. It can look down on us from
up over the edge, surveying the earth it came out of,

the earth that people are made from, who have
trundled wheelbarrows of mud and stone, building
selves that have spread into streets and houses.

For this particular place, which I'm so tired of,
and for my mother, so tired of more than location,
December has come because it always will.

# Acknowledgements and Notes

Poems in this book have been previously published by *Compass*, *Ink Sweat & Tears*, *London Grip*, *New Walk*, *The North*, and *Under the Radar*. 'Pears' was commended in the Hippocrates competition.

I owe this book to Stephen Knight and Goldsmiths where I have been working on a PhD. Essential feedback has also come from a number of workshop groups as well as individual poets, and fifteen poems have come from workshop prompts set by thirteen different people. I won't apologise for being a creature of the poetry workshop culture, but I'm not going to name them all individually.

Thanks to James Grant for the title suggestion, and much else.

Mr Luczinski is my avatar, from my great-grandfather having been Luczinski before changing his name to Daniels. Alan Watts on hurrying and delaying is from *Does it Matter?*

Francis Howgill: see *Quaker Faith & Practice*, §19.08.

Thanks to Sukie de la Croix for the information about Zsa Zsa Gabor's house.

'Riff on a Line of Miłosz' began from staying in the Miłosz room during a Hawthornden Fellowship: the line is from 'Account', translated by Czeslaw Miłosz and Robert Pinsky.

This book has been typeset by
SALT PUBLISHING LIMITED
using Sabon, a font designed by Jan Tschichold
for the D. Stempel AG, Linotype and Monotype Foundries.
It is manufactured using Holmen Book Cream 70gsm,
a Forest Stewardship Council™ certified paper from the
Hallsta Paper Mill in Sweden. It was printed and bound
by Clays Limited in Bungay, Suffolk, Great Britain.

CROMER
GREAT BRITAIN
MMXIX